Outlaws and Lawmen of the Wild West

JESSE JAMES

Carl R. Green

➤ and ◄

William R. Sanford

ENSLOW PUBLISHERS, INC.

44 Fadem Road   P.O. Box 38
Box 699   Aldershot
Springfield, N.J. 07081   Hants GU12 6BP
U.S.A.   U.K.

Library of Congress Cataloging-In-Publication Data

Green, Carl R.
    Jesse James / Carl R. Green and William R. Sanford.
    p. cm. — (Outlaws and lawmen of the wild west)
    Includes bibliographical references and index.
    Summary: A biography of the outlaw who, with his brother Frank,
led a gang of bank and train robbers from the late 1860's through
the 1870's.
    ISBN 0-89490-365-9
    1. James, Jesse, 1847–1882—Juvenile literature. 2. Outlaws—West
(U.S.)—Biography—Juvenile literature. 3. Frontier and pioneer
life—West (U.S.)—Juvenile literature. 4. West (U.S.)—
History—1848–1950—Juvenile literature. [1. James, Jesse, 1847–1882.
2. Robbers and outlaws. 3. West (U.S.)—History.] I. Sanford, William R.
(William Reynolds), 1927– . II. Title. III. Series: Green, Carl R.
Outlaws and lawmen of the wild west.
F594.J2825 1992
364.1'552'092—dc20
[B]   91-18123
                                         CIP
                                         AC

Illustration Credits:
Denver Public Library, Western History Department, pp. 7, 18, 31, 37; Carl
R. Green and William R. Sanford, p. 6; Kansas State Historical Society,
Topeka, Kansas, pp. 13, 14; Library of Congress, pp. 29, 43; Minnesota
Historical Society, p. 32; National Archives, p. 40; State Historical Society
of Missouri, pp. 11, 23, 26, 39, 42; Western History Collections, University
of Oklahoma Library, pp. 25, 44.

CONTENTS

AUTHORS' NOTE

This book tells the story of the outlaw Jesse James. Jesse and his brother Frank were as well-known in the late 1800s as rock stars are today. People all over the country talked about the James boys. The newspapers and magazines of the day printed stories about them. Some were made up, but others were true. The events described in this book all come from firsthand reports.

1

JESSE AND THE WIDOW

Jesse James was an outlaw and a gunslinger. He made his living by robbing banks and trains. Jesse did not think of himself as a bad man. If he shot someone, he did not worry. "The fool should not have tried to stop us," Jesse told his friends.

During the 1800s big business was hated and feared. So what if Jesse robbed banks and trains? That did not upset poor people. Many of them looked up to Jesse as a hero.

The idea that Jesse was a good man grew out of stories that may not be true. Even so, many people believed them. One of the stories is about Jesse and a young widow.

Once, the story goes, Jesse's gang asked for food at a farmhouse. The widow who lived there gave them a fine meal. As he ate, Jesse saw the woman crying. She said

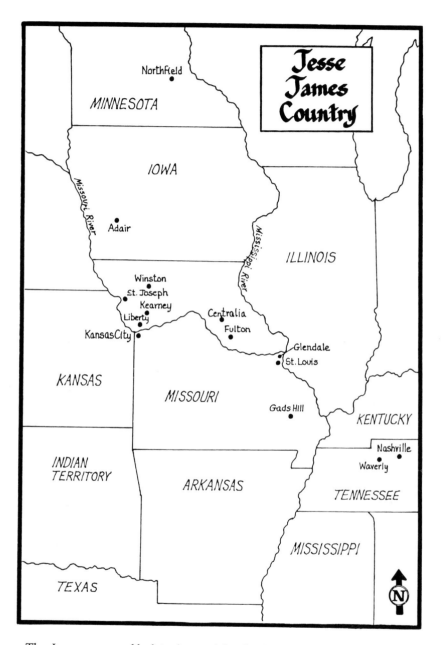

The James gang robbed trains and banks in four states. Jesse's home was at Kearney in western Missouri, but he died in St. Joseph.

that her husband had been killed in the Civil War. Left alone with young children, she could not pay her debts. A heartless banker was coming to take away her farm that same day.

Jesse gave the woman the money she needed. He told her to get a signed receipt from the banker. That will be proof that you paid him, he said. Then he and the boys rode off.

When the banker came, the widow paid him the money. The man was angry. He really wanted her farm. But there was nothing he could do. He took the money and gave her the receipt. Later, when he left the farm, he

Jesse and his gang relax around a campfire after escaping from a posse. Legend says that on a trip like this Jesse helped a widow save her farm.

was stopped by Jesse and his gang, who pointed pistols at him. Jesse took the money back, waved, and rode away.

Is the story true? Most experts say it never happened. Jesse James was not a Robin Hood who stole from the rich and gave to the poor. What he stole, he kept for himself.

JESSE GROWS UP

Much of western Missouri was still raw frontier in the mid-1800s. Life was hard. People were more likely to die of disease or gunshot wounds than of old age. If Jesse James grew up to be a killer, the times helped make him so.

Jesse's father, Robert James, was a preacher. Robert married Zerelda Cole in 1842. The young couple soon moved to a farm near Kearney in western Missouri. Reverend James preached in the New Hope Baptist Church on Sundays. During the week he and Zerelda ran the farm with the help of black slaves.

Frank, the James's first child, was born in 1843. A second son died soon after birth. Jesse Woodson James was born in 1847. His sister, Susan, came two years later.

Reverend James was well liked around Kearney. He found time to help start a college in the area. But he could not resist the call of the gold fields. Robert went West in 1850 to "strike it rich." Three weeks later he fell ill and died.

Zerelda soon wed Ben Simms. But Frank and Jesse refused to obey their stepfather. Simms moved out. In 1855, Zerelda married Dr. Reuben Samuel. Samuel was a gentle man. He let the James boys do what they wished.

Frank, Jesse, and Susan soon had four new brothers and sisters. The children grew up on the Samuel farm. In normal times the boys might have grown up to own their own farms.

But the times were not normal. The people of Missouri were mostly from the South. They wanted to keep slaves. Some of them thought Kansas should be a slave state, too. Fighting broke out when settlers who did not keep slaves moved into Kansas. Armed men from Missouri raided the antislave towns. Houses were burned, and people were killed on both sides.

In 1861 the battles in Kansas became part of a larger Civil War. The South tried to leave the United States. The North went to war to save the Union. Missouri was torn between staying in the Union and joining the South. In the end, the state stayed loyal, but Zerelda's heart was with the South. She cheered when Frank left to join the South's rebel army.

Young Frank soon came down with measles. Captured by Union troops, he gave them his promise not to

Jesse was a teenager when the war began. Like Frank, he shared his mother's belief in the Southern cause.

fight again. That earned him a safe trip home. But the Union general in Missouri ordered all young men to join the state militia. Frank refused to fight against the South. He ran off and joined Quantrill's Raiders.

William Quantrill's raiders did not belong to the regular army. Fighting as guerrillas, they broke all the rules of war. They struck without warning. Their swift attacks burned towns and killed Union soldiers.

Hit-and-run raids damaged the Union army but could not defeat it. Union troops drove the last rebel army from Missouri in 1862. The victory did not end the fighting. Both sides wanted revenge. Riders from Kansas struck Missouri towns that helped the South. With the rebel army gone, it was up to Quantrill and his men to fight back.

When Frank joined Quantrill, the Raiders had less than 250 men. Most were tough young horsemen. Many enjoyed their violent life. They burned bridges and attacked Union patrols. The cost of failure was high. Captured Raiders were shot by firing squads.

The war soon came to the Samuel place. Some Kansas troops rode up and asked Dr. Samuel to help them find Quantrill. The older man refused to talk. That made the troops angry. They put a rope around his neck and hung him from a tree. When Samuel was nearly dead they let him down. Still Samuel would not talk. The soldiers yanked him up again and again. At last they

A Kansas town goes up in flames during a surprise attack by Quantrill's Raiders. The sketch was made by an artist who lived to tell about it. Jesse killed his first man during a similar raid.

gave up. They rode off, leaving the luckless man hanging from the tree. Zerelda saved his life by cutting him down.

The soldiers then found Jesse plowing a field. They asked him the same questions. He refused to talk. The men beat him with a rope. The blows cut into Jesse's back. His shirt was soon stained red with blood.

Jesse was so full of rage he tried to join up with Quantrill. The Raiders turned him down, saying he was too young. But word got out that Jesse had been to see Quantrill. As a result, Zerelda and Susan were put in jail for a few weeks.

When Jesse turned sixteen the Raiders let him join. Bloody Bill Anderson was his captain. Jesse was then a

William Quantrill was a thorn in the side of Union forces during the Civil War. He led tough horsemen in lightning raids on troops, rail lines, and towns. Jesse gained a taste for battle while riding with one of Quantrill's bands.

slim, dark-haired young man who looked like a boy. An old illness made his pale blue eyes blink more often than usual. Despite his looks, Jesse was brave. When he went into battle he fought like a tiger.

Jesse soon earned a nickname. A loaded pistol went off while he was cleaning it. The bullet took off the tip of his left middle finger. Jesse yelled, "That's the dod-dingus pistol I ever saw!" From then on his friends called him Dingus. In the years to come Jesse wore a glove to cover the missing finger tip.

A year later Jesse was shot in the lung. The wound was painful, but it healed fast. Jesse came back in time to take part in a raid on Centralia, Missouri. The Raiders looted the town and shot captured Union soldiers. Fresh Union troops traced the Raiders and attacked their camp. In the battle that followed, Jesse shot the Union commander. It was his first killing.

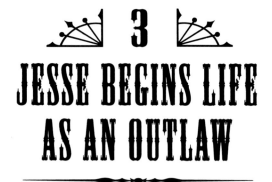

3
JESSE BEGINS LIFE AS AN OUTLAW

Centralia was Bloody Bill Anderson's last big battle. After that, the Raiders broke up under Union pressure. Jesse joined a group of men who moved south to Texas. They spent the winter there.

The Civil War was coming to a close. The South's Robert E. Lee laid down his arms in April 1865. One by one the other rebel armies gave up. Frank James and the last few Raiders rode into Kentucky with Quantrill. They hoped to escape the firing squad by giving up there. But Quantrill was killed before he could surrender. Frank and the others turned themselves in.

The news that the war had ended was slow to reach Texas. When it came, the Raiders there knew it was time to give up. But would the North treat them fairly?

Jesse and the others headed north. As they neared Lexington, Missouri, Jesse rode ahead. He carried a white flag to show that he was unarmed. But the first Union troops he met opened fire. A bullet knocked Jesse from his horse. He tried to escape by crawling into the woods. Union soldiers chased him, eager for the kill. They turned back when Jesse shot one of their horses.

Jesse was soon burning with fever. He spent the night in a cool creek. The next day he woke up weak and in pain. A farm worker found him and took him to town. After a doctor treated his chest wound a Union major came to see him. The major took pity on the young man. He paid a wagon driver to take Jesse home.

Jesse was near death when he reached his mother in Nebraska. Zerelda had moved there after she and the younger children were forced to leave Kearney. She nursed her son for eight long weeks. Despite her care, the wound was slow to heal.

Although he was in pain, Jesse wanted to go home. He said he did not want to die in a Northern state. Zerelda helped him board a steamboat. In Kansas City, Jesse was nursed by a cousin, Zee Mimms. Zee and Jesse fell in love and planned to wed. But first he had to regain his health.

Thanks to Zee, Jesse was soon well enough to travel. A wagon carried him back to the Samuel place. Dr. Samuel and Frank were already there, working the farm. Safe on his home soil, Jesse grew strong again. One by one, a gang of friends from the war days joined him. None of them were looking for honest work.

As Jesse's wounds healed, he made plans for his future. The hard life of a farmer was not for him. He decided to live by his guns, just as he had during the war. Robbing banks and trains might lead to jail or an early grave. But a life of crime could also lead to quick and easy money.

The young outlaw said he would go where the money was. By that, he meant he would rob banks. This was a new idea. In those days people thought banks were as safe as churches. No one dreamed of robbing banks except during wartime.

Jesse and Frank pose with pistols drawn for this rare tintype. The two brothers liked to have their pictures taken.

All that changed on February 13, 1866. Jesse picked Liberty, Missouri as his first target. He knew the town well. It was only a dozen miles from the Samuel place.

Ten men rode into Liberty on that cold winter morning. They halted their horses in front of the Clay County Savings Bank. Two of the men jumped down and walked into the bank. A third man held the horses. His friends kept lookout.

The bank had just opened. Cashier Greenup Bird and his son William looked up when the men walked in. One bearded man warmed his hands at the stove. The second man asked for change for a ten dollar bill. Before Greenup could move the man drew a gun. "I'd like all the money in the bank," he said. Greenup never said so, but he may have known the man was Jesse.

The second gunman was aiming a pistol at William. "Make a noise and we will shoot you down," he said.

The outlaws led the two Birds back to the vault. They knew the money was kept in that iron strong room. William Bird was forced to scoop gold and silver coins into a wheat sack. The second man emptied a tin box that stood on the cashier's desk. The sack was soon filled with over $60,000 in cash and bonds.

The outlaws pushed the Birds into the vault and slammed the door. "Stay in there! Don't you know all Birds should be caged?" the leader yelled. Laughing at their own joke, the gunmen ran out to their horses.

The gang filled the air with gunfire as they rode out

of town. The wild shots sent people ducking for safety. A college student named George Wymore did not duck fast enough. One of the outlaws killed him with four quick shots.

The gang headed south, stopping only to split the money. They threw away the bonds they could not turn into cash. Riding fast, they crossed the Missouri River by ferry, then broke up. Back in Liberty, men formed a posse to chase the gang. But they lost the outlaws' trail in the snow.

The posse did not visit the Samuel place. The few people who had seen Jesse and Frank that morning kept quiet. They knew the James boys would kill anyone who talked to the sheriff.

4

JESSE JAMES, TRAIN ROBBER

After his first bank robbery, Jesse robbed at least seven more banks. The gang hit banks in three states. They even held up the box office at the Kansas City Fair.

Banks were not the only target for the James boys. Jesse and Frank also robbed trains. That was a popular move. Many people hated the railroads. High freight rates made it hard for farmers to make a profit. They asked for laws that would control the railroads. But the railroad owners paid lawmakers to vote against the laws.

The Reno brothers pulled the first train robbery in 1866. Seven years later, Jesse and Frank held up their first train. Stopping trains was risky, but the James boys had learned how in the war. Jesse picked the Chicago, Rock Island & Pacific to rob. Frank had heard that one of the line's trains carried a safe full of gold. Jesse made plans to stop that train near Adair, Iowa.

Jesse told his gang to pull up one of the rails. He knew the train would stop if the track was torn up. The engineer saw the danger, but put on the brakes too late. The engine tipped over, crushing him. Two masked robbers ran up and forced the mail car clerk to open the safe. They found only $2,000 inside. The gold was on a train due to pass the next day.

The gang also robbed the people who were riding on the train. They took watches, money, and jewels. Some stories said that Jesse did not steal from pretty women. That was not true. Jesse stole from anyone who had something he wanted.

The James boys were among the first outlaws to hold up trains. These risky holdups did not make them rich. After stopping a train they often found very little money in the mail car safe.

The James gang robs a train and its passengers. Jesse had a quick trigger finger during these holdups. He killed those who did not obey quickly enough.

In 1874 the gang stopped a train at Gads Hill, Missouri. They robbed the passengers, cut open the mail sacks, and cleaned out the safe. The gang rode away with more than ten thousand dollars.

Before riding off, Jesse gave a note to a trainman. It was a story for the newspapers. The headline read, "THE MOST DARING ROBBERY ON RECORD." Jesse had written the story to make sure the papers got the facts straight. He liked to read about his crimes.

After a holdup, the train crew often asked local farmers to form a posse. The reply would come back, "Go chase 'em yourself. It ain't my money they stole." A few posses were formed. They gave up when the trail led to Clay County. The local people knew better than to go after Jesse and Frank.

By now the outlaws had friends all over Missouri. Many people were still angry over losing the Civil War. Outlaws who robbed Northern banks and trains became heroes. Jesse's growing fame brought new recruits for the gang. The best known were the three Younger brothers.

The outlaws needed friends. It helped to know farmers who would give them a meal and a place to sleep. In the morning the outlaws paid for their stay with gold. The coins made the farmers smile. They could work all year and not see that much money.

When they left, the leader would shake the farmer's hand. "You know, I'm Jesse James," he liked to say.

The banks and railroads wanted to hang Jesse, not shake his hand. When lawmen could not catch Jesse, the owners turned elsewhere. In 1871 a bank hired the Pinkerton Detective Agency. Robert Pinkerton followed the gang's trail almost to Kearney. Then he turned back. There were too many people willing to lie for the James boys, he said.

The Pinkertons did not give up. In 1874, a young agent showed up in Liberty. John Whicher bragged that he was going to capture Jesse and Frank. Despite his soft hands and city ways he claimed to be a farmer. His goal was to get a job at the Samuel place so he could spy on

Jesse. A few days later Whicher's body was found near Kearney. He had been shot through the heart.

That spring Jesse and Zee Mimms agreed to wed. The cousins had been in love for nine years. The families were against the marriage, but Jesse and Zee would not listen. They were married in April by Jesse's uncle.

Zerelda Samuel was the mother of the James boys. She went to her grave without admitting that Jesse and Frank were outlaws.

PROCLAMATION

$5,000⁰⁰

REWARD

FOR EACH of SEVEN ROBBERS of THE TRAIN at WINSTON,MO.,JULY 15,1881, and THE MURDER of CONDUCTER WESTFALL

$ 5,000.00

ADDITIONAL for ARREST or CAPTURE

DEAD OR ALIVE
OF JESSE OR FRANK JAMES

THIS NOTICE TAKES the PLACE of ALL PREVIOUS REWARD NOTICES.
CONTACT SHERIFF, DAVIESS COUNTY, MISSOURI IMMEDIATELY
T. T. CRITTENDEN, GOVERNOR
STATE OF MISSOURI
JULY 26, 1881

Posters like these promised a big reward for the capture of Jesse and Frank.

The new husband had a price on his head. One bank had put up $3,000 for his capture. The railroads added $5,000. This was big money when men worked twelve hours a day for one dollar.

The reward money brought the Pinkertons back. In early 1875, nine agents sneaked up on the Samuel place. They found two sweaty horses in the barn. That made them think Frank and Jesse were in the house. One man lit the fuse of a kerosene bomb and threw it into the kitchen. Dr. Samuel tried to kick the bomb into the fireplace. He was too late. The blast killed nine-year-old Archie and injured Zerelda. A few days later a doctor had to cut off her arm.

Were Frank and Jesse home that day? No one knows for sure. They may have jumped from an upstairs room to escape. What is sure is that someone opened fire. The Pinkertons ran off. One of the agents was wounded and died soon afterward.

The public was angry, but not with the James gang. Jesse did not harm women or kill children, did he?

Nothing seemed to stop Jesse and Frank. The robberies went on—banks, trains, and stagecoaches. Governor Thomas Crittenden said he would rid the state of the outlaws. He put up $5,000 for the capture of the James boys. But Jesse's luck turned bad long before anyone could collect the reward.

5

DISASTER AT NORTHFIELD

By 1876 Jesse and Frank had pulled off a long string of holdups. Even so, many people still believed in them. Their friends said the James boys were honest men. Their only crime, it was said, was having ridden with Quantrill. Newspapers helped by printing Jesse's letters. In them he always claimed he was somewhere else when the holdups took place.

But more facts were coming out. Hobbs Kerry was captured after the gang robbed a train. Hobbs talked freely. He named Jesse, Frank, and the Younger brothers as gang members.

Autumn of 1876 also brought new troubles. Jesse led seven gang members north to check out the banks in Minnesota. He picked a bank in Northfield as his target.

Jesse, Bob Younger, and Sam Wells reached the bank first. They watched Cole Younger stop in the middle of

28

Cole and Bob Younger (standing) pose with Jesse (seated center) and Frank. For a time the Youngers were almost as famous as the James brothers. They were captured after the Northfield bank holdup.

the street. Cole looked as though he was fixing his saddle. Clell Miller joined Jesse and the four outlaws walked into the bank. Frank, Jim Younger, and Bill Chadwell stayed back to guard the escape.

Trouble started when Clell failed to stop a man from leaving the bank. The man ran off, shouting that the bank was being robbed. A store owner grabbed his rifle and opened fire. Frank and his two friends galloped toward the bank, pistols drawn. Bullets were soon whizzing around their heads. A dozen or so Northfield men had opened fire.

Inside the bank, things were also going badly. Bank clerk Joseph Heywood tried to slam the vault door on Sam Wells. Sam barely escaped being shut inside the vault. Jesse then ordered Heywood to open the safe. The clerk pointed to a time lock. The safe cannot be opened, he said. In truth, the safe was unlocked, but Jesse did not have time to check. A second clerk ran out the back door. Wells shot him in the arm, but the man kept on running.

Jesse heard the gunfire in the street. He knew it was time to go. On the way out he shot the helpless Heywood.

Chadwell and Miller lay dead in the street. Frank had a leg wound. Cole and Jim Younger had both been hit. Cole pulled Bob Younger up behind him and the gang fled. Behind them church bells rang the alarm.

Day after day a posse chased the gang. When their horses wore out the outlaws stole fresh ones. After

Jesse and his gang shot a number of bank clerks. During the Northfield holdup, Jesse killed one clerk and Sam Wells wounded a second.

several days they split up. Jesse and Frank escaped into Iowa. A week later the posse caught up with the others. Sam Wells died in a fierce gun battle. The three Youngers were captured and put in jail.

His failure at Northfield upset Jesse. For the first time, the people of a town had turned on him. It seemed best to lie low and wait for better times.

Jesse and Frank slowly worked their way back home. Frank went to Fulton to have his wound cared for. That same night, Frank's doctor and Jesse ate in the town's hotel. One story says they shared a table with some Pinkerton men. The Pinkertons were looking for the James brothers, but no one gave Jesse away. Cool as always, Jesse very likely enjoyed the close call.

Jesse and Frank moved on to a hideout in Texas. They

called it their Rest Ranch. Frank settled in with his books, but Jesse was restless. It is likely that he led Frank on trips into Mexico. On one trip, they ran into some soldiers who wanted the reward money. But Jesse and Frank shot their way out of the trap.

Jesse did not like shootouts. He knew he was not a good shot. He once fired six times at a man—and missed every time. When he did kill a man it was from close range.

By now Jesse and Zee had a son, Jesse Edwards

An early artist made this drawing of the Northfield bank robbery. The men of the town killed two of Jesse's men in a wild shootout. Later, a posse hunted down all but Frank and Jesse.

James. When the brothers came back from Texas they packed their wives and children into wagons. Their route led them to Tennessee, a trip of 500 miles. In August 1877, Jesse found a home in Waverly. Frank lived a long day's ride away in Nashville.

Jesse used the name J. D. Howard. He joined the church and sang in the choir. When the county fair opened, he raced his horse, Red Fox. Red Fox won a number of races for his proud owner. Zee gave birth to twins, but the babies died soon after birth. Jesse lived on a farm, but he still did not like hard work. He paid his bills with money from his holdups.

The money ran low after two years. Jesse moved Zee and the baby to a house in Nashville. His neighbors thought he was in the wheat business. When little Jesse was four, Zee gave birth to a baby girl. They named her Mary.

Frank worked for a lumber company. He saved his money and rented a farm where he raised hogs and horses. Jesse and his family joined Frank on the farm. But Jesse could not stay in one place for long. He took off to visit a friend in New Mexico.

When Jesse came back Frank said he was tired of the outlaw life. He told Jesse they could make their living by working the farm. Jesse turned him down. He was ready to go back to his real "work"—robbing banks and trains.

6

THE END OF THE TRAIL

Jesse's first job was to find a new gang. The old gang was out of action. The Younger brothers were in prison. Sam Wells and Bill Chadwell were dead. Clell Miller's bones were hanging in a Northfield doctor's office.

The word went out that Jesse needed men. Ed Miller, Clell's brother, joined up. Then Wood Hite, Jesse's cousin, signed on. Tucker Bassham, Bill Ryan, and Dick Liddil also joined.

The new James gang pulled its first job in the fall of 1879. Glendale, Missouri was the target. When they arrived the outlaws found most of the townfolk in Glendale's one store. At gunpoint, the gang herded their captives to the train station. Jesse smashed the telegraph while the others laid logs on the track. When the train braked to a stop the gang took six thousand dollars from the mail car. Before he left, Jesse told the men on the train who he was. Jesse James was back!

Jesse gave each gang member his share. Then he made the long ride back to Nashville. A few people must have wondered where he had been. But none of them knew that the quiet Mr. Howard was really Jesse James.

The new gang soon fell apart. Tucker Bassham bragged too loudly that he was part of the James gang. When captured, he confessed that he had taken part in the Glendale holdup. Later, Bill Ryan was put on trial for the same crime. Tucker won his freedom by naming Ryan as part of the gang.

This setback did not stop Jesse. In the fall of 1880 he and a friend robbed a stagecoach in Kentucky. The two men rode off with a gold watch, a diamond ring, and some cash.

Then Frank had a change of heart. He rejoined the gang the next July. Jesse had a new plan ready. Gang members bought tickets on the train they planned to rob. They were all on board when the train left the station. Jesse pulled his gun and shouted a signal. Everyone froze, but he fired anyway. His bullet killed the conductor. At the same time his men were forcing their way into the mail car. They shot a man who looked as though he was trying to escape. Then they cleaned out the safe.

Nothing seemed to be going right. The gang had killed two men—but gained only $800. Gang member

Ed Miller dropped from sight a few weeks later. People said that Jesse may have killed him for talking too much.

The gang's last train job nearly ended in a wreck. Jesse stopped a train he thought was carrying a large sack of cash. Instead, the safe was nearly empty. With the train stopped, a second train came chugging down the same track. A brakeman ran up the track and stopped the oncoming train just in time. Jesse gave the man a tip. He also gave the engineer two silver dollars to drink to his health.

Frank did not like the way things were going. He left the gang in the spring of 1882 and went back to his farm. The brothers never saw each other again.

Jesse was 34 years old when Frank left the gang. He moved Zee and the children to St. Joseph, Missouri.

A quick-thinking trainman flags down an oncoming train. His own train was being robbed by Jesse and his gang. If the second train had not stopped, both trains would have been wrecked.

Jesse thought of holdups as his "business." If he was short of cash he found a bank, train, or stagecoach to rob. Here, Jesse and a friend strip five men of their wallets and watches.

They lived in a white house on a hill. Jesse used the name Thomas Howard and grew a beard.

With his cash almost gone, Jesse planned to rob a bank in Platte City. He said he could do the job with a three-man gang. Zee thought he wanted the money to buy a farm.

Charlie Ford, a new member of the gang, liked the plan. In late March, Jesse and Charlie met with Charlie's brother, Bob Ford. Bob said he would join them for the Platte City robbery. Later he took Charlie aside. He said they should kill Jesse and claim the reward. Charlie agreed.

No one knows the whole story. Rumors said that Governor Crittenden and two police officers cut a deal with the Fords. Charlie and Bob agreed to give them three-fourths of the $10,000 reward. In return, the officials promised to keep the Fords out of jail.

On April 3 the Fords joined Jesse and Zee for breakfast. Jesse gave Bob a new pistol and Charlie a new horse. Why did he trust the Fords? Most experts agree that Jesse must have known the Fords would try to kill him. He had already caught Bob Ford lying to him. And there was the reward. It was so large and tempting.

In the old days Jesse would have driven the Fords out of his house. But now he was tired. The law was closing in on him. If he was caught he would be locked up. That was too much to bear. Jesse had always said, "They can kill me, but they will never send me to jail."

When the men moved to the living room, Jesse took off his guns. He turned his back on the Fords, saying that a picture needed dusting. As he climbed up on a chair Bob and Charlie moved in behind him. Bob raised his new pistol. The click of the gun being cocked made Jesse turn his head. Bob knew it was now or never. He pulled the trigger.

The bullet hit Jesse in the back of the head. He was dead when he crashed to the floor.

Zee rushed in from the kitchen. She screamed with rage and grief when she saw Jesse. The Fords ran out. Bob sent a telegram to the governor. It read: "I've got him, sure."

Bob and Charlie were tried and sentenced to death. But the officials kept their word. Governor Crittenden gave the killers a full pardon. What the Fords could not escape was the hatred of the public. Bob Ford was always known as "that dirty little coward that shot Mr. Howard."

Bob Ford takes aim at the back of Jesse's head. Jesse's guns lie on the table and his wife is busy in the kitchen. Ford pulled the trigger a moment later.

Bob Ford poses with the gun he used to kill Jesse James. Ford did not go to jail, but he paid a high price for his crime. Until he died he was known as "the dirty little coward who shot Mr. Howard."

7

THE ROBIN HOOD MYTH

Bob Ford killed Jesse James but he could not kill Jesse's myth. The stories grew as the years passed. Songs were written that turned the outlaw into a hero. One song told it this way:

> *Jesse James was one of his names,*
> *Another it was Howard.*
> *He robbed the rich of every stitch.*
> *You bet, he was no coward.*

Frank James outlived his brother by more than thirty years. He was put on trial for his crimes—and was set free by the jury. Frank helped build Jesse's myth by telling his own tall tales of their lives. He even charged fifty cents to visit the Samuel place.

Why did the outlaw Jesse James become a hero? The feelings left by the Civil War helped build the myth.

Frank James cashed in on his fame when he was an old man. Here he charges fifty cents to visit the farm where he and Jesse once lived.

Many people in the South said that Jesse was righting the wrongs done to them. Magazines called dime novels added to the myth. They ran story after story about Jesse. Most of the stories were fiction, but no one cared. Readers liked stories about outlaw heroes.

It was also true that Americans like underdogs. The myth said that Jesse stole from the rich. That turned him into a home-grown Robin Hood. If this Robin Hood kept what he stole, no one seemed to care. People liked to see

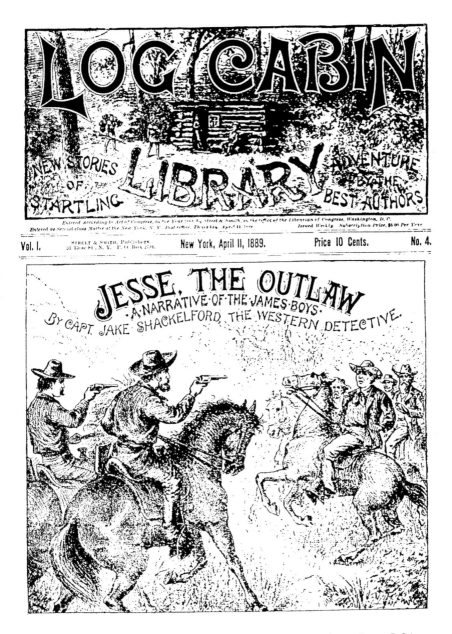

Entered According to Act of Congress, in the Year 1889, by Street & Smith, in the office of the Librarian of Congress, Washington, D. C.
Entered as Second class Matter at the New York, N. Y. Post office, Thursday April 11, 1889.

Issued Weekly. Subscription Price, $5.00 Per Year

Vol. I. STREET & SMITH, Publishers, 31 Rose St., N. Y. P. O. Box 2734.   New York, April 11, 1889.   Price 10 Cents.   No. 4.

Dime novels helped turn Jesse James into an outlaw hero. Log Cabin Library put Jesse on this cover because stories about him sold magazines. Most of the stories were more fiction than fact.

the rich and powerful taken down a peg. A second verse of the song added:

> *Jesse stole from the rich*
> *And he gave to the poor.*
> *He'd a hand and a heart and a brain.*

Was Jesse a sinner or a hero? Was he a cruel killer or a loving family man? Perhaps he was some of each. The whole truth may never be known.

GLOSSARY

Civil War—The war between the North and South, 1861–1865.

detective agency—A business that provides police services for anyone who pays its fees.

dime novels—Low-cost magazines that printed popular fiction during the late 1800s.

frontier—A region that is just being opened to settlement. Life in a frontier area is often hard and dangerous.

guerrillas—Small, fast-moving military forces that operate outside the normal rules of warfare.

gunslingers—Outlaws and lawmen of the Wild West who settled arguments with their pistols.

militia—Lightly-trained citizens who are called to military duty to back up the regular army.

myth—A story that many people believe but which is almost always untrue.

Pinkertons—Private detectives who worked for the famous Pinkerton Detective Agency.

posse—A group of citizens who join with law enforcement officers to aid in the capture of outlaws.

Quantrill's Raiders—A band of Southern guerrillas led by William Quantrill who fought against Union forces in Missouri.

Union—The name given to the United States forces that fought against the South during the Civil War.

MORE GOOD READING ABOUT JESSE JAMES

Bradley, Larry C. *Jesse James: The Making of a Legend*. Nevada, Mo.: Larren Pubs., 1980.

Breihan, Carl W. *The Day Jesse James Was Killed*. Hollywood, Fla.: Fell Pubs., 1961.

Horan, James D. "The James-Younger Gang," *The Authentic Wild West: The Outlaws*. New York: Crown Publishers, 1977, pp. 29–146.

Settle, William A. *Jesse James Was His Name; or Fact and Fiction Concerning the Careers of the Notorious James Brothers of Missouri*. Columbia, Mo.: University of Missouri Press, 1966.

Steele, Philip W. *Jesse and Frank James: The Family History*. Gretna, La.: Pelican, 1987.

Trachtman, Paul and the Editors of Time-Life Books. "Buccaneers of the Border States," *The Gunfighters*. Alexandria, Va.: Time-Life Books, 1974, pp. 52–89.

INDEX

921
JAMES
GRE

Green, Carl R.

Jesse James.

2742

$14.95

DATE